STRATEGICALLY   SUITED

STRATEGICALLY SUITED

Your Secret Edge to Grow Sales and Get New Clients

LEE HEYWARD

NEW YORK

NASHVILLE • MELBOURNE • VANCOUVER

Strategically Suited

Your Secret Edge to Grow Sales and Get New Clients

Published in New York, New York, by Morgan James Publishing in partnership with Difference Press. Morgan James is a trademark of Morgan James, LLC. www.MorganJamesPublishing.com

The Morgan James Speakers Group can bring authors to your live event. For more information or to book an event visit The Morgan James Speakers Group at www.TheMorganJamesSpeakersGroup.com.

ISBN 978-1-68350-243-2 paperback
ISBN 978-1-68350-244-9 eBook
Library of Congress Control Number: 2016915452

Interior Design by:
Chris Treccani
www.3dogdesign.net

In an effort to support local communities, raise awareness and funds, Morgan James Publishing donates a percentage of all book sales for the life of each book to Habitat for Humanity Peninsula and Greater Williamsburg.

Get involved today! Visit
www.MorganJamesBuilds.com

TABLE OF CONTENTS

Introduction: Your Secret Sales Weapon   xi

The Fake Cowgirl   xiii
I'll Wear My Own Shoes   xiv
What's Possible?   xvi

Chapter 1: You Are What You Wear   1
Your Mental Edge   3
You Never Get a Second Chance to Make a First Impression 5
Thin Slicing   6
The Impression of Increase   8
Million-Dollar Shoes   11
First Impressions Are a Sales Opportunity, Even if You've
    Already Made the Sale   13
The Bird Shit Lawyer   14
What Are People Really Buying?   17
Your Image Is Your Personal Brand   20
Does Your Image Match Your Opportunities?   23

Chapter 2: Gain an Edge in Your Business   27

   Your Business EDGE   29

   Engage Your Ideal Client: 31

   Dress As If: 35

   Get Real: 38

   Every Day: Commit to Consistency: 41

   Consistency Is Powerful Positioning   43

   When It's Right, Consistency Is Easy   46

Chapter 3: Can New Clothes Really Make You More Money?   49

   The ROI of Investing in Yourself   50

   The Trickle-Down Effect   53

   Impeccable Is the Standard   55

   When You Invest More, You Buy Less   56

   Investing in Yourself Gives You a Psychological Advantage 58

   The Key to ROI Is Your Decision   60

Chapter 4: The Trap of the Perfectly Good   63

   The Race to $1 Million   66

   Thank Goodness, It Fits!   67

   Time Marches On   72

   Anyone Can Help You Be Perfectly Good   74

   What's the Truth?   75

Chapter 5: The Freedom of Success   79
    The Real Point of This Book   81
    The Surprise Secret   83

Afterword: Taking the Next Step   87

Acknowledgments   89

About the Author   93

Thank You   95

INTRODUCTION

Your Secret Sales Weapon

Some time during my senior year of college, I bought a suit. I didn't have an interview I needed it for; I just thought, I'm a college senior, and seniors are supposed to find a job–so obviously, I need a suit. It was a double-breasted pantsuit with navy pinstripes. I'm sure it was very cool at the time.

I was graduating from college. I had a suit. I was ready to conquer the real world!

Then, after graduation, I landed a dream job as a visual merchandiser for Ariat International, an equestrian footwear and apparel company. It was especially exciting, because I have ridden horses since the age of five. When I interviewed for the job, I flew to the Atlanta airport, met my soon-to-be boss in the Sky Club during his layover, and was hired on the spot. No suit needed.

As a visual merchandiser, I flew all around the country to help our accounts sell Ariat's product line. I visited national accounts as well as smaller, locally owned stores. That suit I bought would have been ridiculous in an equestrian retail setting. So it hung in the closet, unworn.

When I got my job, I thought merchandising would be fun, and it was. But I had no idea how many ways it would teach me that the way you present what you're selling–as well as the way you present yourself–has a direct correlation with the sales results you get.

I got to be around horse people and horse stuff, and was working for the best company in the equestrian industry. I couldn't have been happier. And not long into the job, I discovered that the business perspective it offered was very interesting as well. I quickly figured out why Ariat hires an entire team of people devoted solely to merchandising. Ariat places a premium on visual merchandising because the company knows it makes all the difference between strong and flat sales.

The stores that were beautifully merchandised and consistently serviced sold two times the amount of product than the stores that haphazardly displayed things wherever there was a spot. The stores that created intentional displays had a considerable edge over the stores without a plan–the latter struggled to get the sales results they wanted, and complained about their business all the time.

The Fake Cowgirl

One day, I found myself at a rodeo where I was helping one of our accounts sell Ariat product. I had been urged to dress the part, which meant dressing like a "cowgirl" in Wrangler jeans, a button-down shirt, a cowboy hat, and cowboy boots. None of it made sense for my personality or level of equestrian expertise, and all of it made me feel as if I were dressing up for Halloween.

I'd already seen how presenting the product a certain way could dramatically increase sales. So I was really interested to see what would happen if I dressed a certain way. Would it, too, increase sales?

I knew instinctively that when it comes to the "merchandising" of yourself, or how you present yourself, it's not as simple as putting on a costume simply to dress the part. In fact, wearing something that feels like a costume will actually detract from your sales.

If I dressed like a cowgirl, any real cowboy would know that I was simply wearing something to be more like them. I could better serve potential buyers as an expert who was approachable and knowledgeable about the product I was selling, while simultaneously appreciative of their sport.

So, at the rodeo, I wore my own clothes and added a western flair. We sold out—no costume—or pinstriped pantsuit—necessary.

I'll Wear My Own Shoes

Fast-forward a year to when I was promoted as a sales representative for the same company. I'm a girl in my early twenties taking over accounts from a very established cowboy who everyone loves. And someone says to me, *Man I'd hate to try and fill Glen's shoes. How are you going to do that?* I said, *I'm not. I'll wear my own shoes.*

In that moment, I had to figure out how to walk into an arena where I wasn't quite like everyone else with 100% confidence in my own sales abilities. Yet in order to succeed, I also had to give my new customer the confidence they needed, to know I was the gal that would help grow their business.

I worked for Ariat for five years and quickly became one of their top sales representatives. I still loved the job when I left, but I didn't want to live life on the road anymore. Often times when I'd drive from account to account, I'd daydream about what I wanted to do next. As it turns out, I'd been training for "the rest of my life" my entire life!

When I was in fourth grade, my best friend started at a new school. I decided we had to make sure that she would arrive at the new school as a "cool kid." So we had a sleepover, and created outfits for the first five days of school. In my mind, this was foolproof. Cool clothes equal cool kid. What more could you want, right?

And it worked. She made friends easily. Clearly, I had a knack for this—but it wasn't until working for Ariat that it all clicked for me.

I finally took a good, hard look at that suit I bought my senior year of college, which had stayed, neglected and unworn, in my closet for years. As it turned out, that suit was something I thought I SHOULD buy, not something that truly served me as a strategic way to get the business results I was after.

I got rid of my suit.

Now, not everyone should get rid of their suit. That's my story. For you, it may be strategic to wear a great suit. Or it may not. There's true power in figuring out which clothing to wear in order to gain an edge in your business, and ultimately increase your bottom line.

What's Possible?

You're successful. You know how to get dressed. You listened when people talked about dressing for success. But now it's time to take it to the next level and discover how changing your clothes will actually increase your sales results.

What could happen if you up-level the way you present yourself? What could happen if simply by getting dressed, you could easily land any opportunity that came your way?

Look at it this way: you're already getting dressed every day. So why not put on clothes that give you an edge in your business, and easily help you grow your bottom line? In my world, that's a secret weapon. And all you have to do to activate it is change your clothes.

CHAPTER 1

You Are What You Wear

My fourth-grade friend, dressed like a "cool kid," felt like a "cool kid," and was perceived as a super cool fourth grader. Now I'm sure a big part of this was because she simply IS an amazing human being, but even at 10 years old, wearing what felt like "cool kid clothes" was like buying an insurance policy.

You and I both know the secret to her success as a cool fourth grader: she believed she could BE a cool fourth grader based on how we prepped her for it. Her new friends weren't just reacting to her clothes. They were reacting to how she felt in those clothes.

Similarly, dressing in a way that gives you the secret edge to sales isn't just about dressing for your client or to make the best first impression. All of that definitely matters, and I'll get into that in just a moment.

Dressing strategically, whether you're in fourth grade or in your fourth year in business, is about how you appear to your client, but it's also about how you appear to yourself. You're dressing to feel a certain way in order to get a specific result.

Frequently, my clients tell me that they used to do sales calls in whatever they happened to be wearing, but after up-leveling their image, they now get dressed and wear clothes that actually change their mental state. They feel powerful and more confident in their ability to serve their client. It comes across—even when they're talking on the phone.

That's an important thing to remember as you read this book. The way you think about yourself—your self-concept—is driving every result you get both personally and professionally. There are a thousand different ways that you can use your image to increase your bottom line, but the key is to start by dressing for yourself. For your own mental advantage. Your mental edge.

Your Mental Edge

When you put on clothing that makes you feel like you can conquer the world, you gain something that only you can give yourself. It's completely unique to you. It's a mental edge over the way you were even just seconds before you put those clothes on.

Rhonda Rousey, one of the Ultimate Fighting Championship's highest paid fighters, does her own hair before every fight. Why is this remarkable? Because she has a team of people dedicated to helping her win. They are responsible for making sure that every possible thing she might need to think about or do is taken care of–including, theoretically, styling her hair. Her job is to rest, fuel her body, and go into the ring and win. But it turns out that a task as unremarkable as doing her own hair is actually one of the most important ways she prepares to win a fight. She does it the same way every time. She always does it alone. And it is the single action that she says transforms her into her fighting mindset. When her fight hair is done, she has her mental edge. She knows she can win.

In 2007, I started my business to help entrepreneurs increase sales simply by up-leveling the way they present themselves. Two years later, I was rolling along with quite a few clients, but my business wasn't growing as quickly as I had hoped. One day, I was talking with success coach David Neagle, my mentor at the time, and he said, "Lee, you always look great, but I'm curious why you dress the way you do."

I had an answer to this. I'd really thought about it. I wanted to dress in an approachable way. I felt that being approachable would be the best way to attract clients. And I wasn't wrong. Approachability is always important. But David then asked if I would dress the same way if I had already achieved the sales results I wanted in my business. The answer was NO. I would have more fun. I would be more badass. I would be quirkier. I would dress more like ME!

I went home and immediately switched to dressing as the "successful me." That same year, I tripled my income.

All I did was change my clothes—and that dramatically changed my income. The real impact was due to the mental edge I instilled in myself. And I know that's exactly why David asked me the question he did, to help me find my edge. To help me have 110% confidence in myself.

I tripled my sales because my own self-concept changed. I knew I could help more people, but I wasn't packaged to stand out. By dressing as the successful me, I was properly merchandised, like Ariat boots. Now, not only was I confident in my abilities, but so was my potential client.

You Never Get a Second Chance to Make a First Impression

You've heard a thousand times how important it is to make a good first impression.

But in my experience, your first impression is your first sales opportunity. Everyone you meet may not be a potential client, but they might be, or they might know someone who is. The way you present yourself sets you up for sales success no matter where you go.

Let's start by talking about first impressions. Upon meeting someone for the first time, the impression you make on them is formed in seven seconds. 1-2-3-4-5-6-7. That's not a lot of time.

Typically in seven seconds, you haven't even had an opportunity to open your mouth and speak. Research has shown that the impression you make on someone is mostly made up of your appearance and nonverbal cues.

A Harvard study conducted by psychologists Nalini Ambady and Robert Rosenthal rated college professors based on one group of students' first impression, and then another group of students' impression after having them as a professor for an entire semester. The first group only watched 10-second video clips of the professors with no sound in order to form their impression. The second group took their class for an entire semester. The study showed that the first impression made from 10 seconds of silent video created almost the same impression as that gleaned from students who had an entire semester to form an opinion about the professor.

Thin Slicing

Ambady and Rosenthal's study created a term called "thin slicing." It means you make very quick inferences about the state, characteristics, or details of an individual or situation with minimal, or thin slices, of information. Judgments made by thin-slicing are often as accurate–and sometimes more accurate–than judgments made over a long period of time.

Genetically, we are hard-wired to make quick decisions–everything from how much you feel you should trust someone to whether or not to buy a certain house.

These decisions are made in a matter of seconds by a type of unconscious thinking called rapid cognition. Malcolm Gladwell wrote an entire book about this called *Blink*. It's all about the kind of thinking that happens in the blink of an eye. In fact, his entire book was inspired by police officers stopping him because they thought he was someone else.

When Gladwell was asked in an interview about where the idea for *Blink* came from, this is what he said:

"Believe it or not, it's because I decided, a few years ago, to grow my hair long. If you look at the author photo on my last book, *The Tipping Point*, you'll see that it used to be cut very short and conservatively. But, on a whim, I let it grow wild, as it had been when I was teenager. Immediately, in very small but significant ways, my life changed. I started getting speeding tickets all the time–and I had never gotten any before. I started getting pulled out of airport security lines for special attention. And one day, while walking along 14th Street in downtown Manhattan, a police van pulled up on the sidewalk, and three officers jumped out. They were looking, as it turned out, for a rapist, and the rapist, they said, looked a lot like me. They pulled out the sketch and the description. I looked at it, and pointed out to them as nicely as I could that in fact the rapist looked nothing at all like me. He was much taller, and much heavier, and about fifteen years younger (and, I added, in a largely futile attempt at humor, not nearly as good-looking.) All we had in common was a large head of curly hair. After twenty minutes or so, the officers finally agreed with me, and let me go. On a scale of things, I realize this was a trivial misunderstanding. African-Americans in the United States suffer indignities far worse than this all the time. But what struck me was how even more subtle and absurd the stereotyping was in my case: this wasn't about something really obvious like skin color, or age, or height, or weight. It was just about hair. Something about the first impression created by my hair derailed every other consideration in the hunt for the rapist, and the impression formed in those first two seconds exerted a powerful hold over the officers' thinking over the next twenty minutes. That episode on the street got me thinking about the weird power of first impressions."

The Impression of Increase

There's nothing hard about dressing in a way that attracts opportunity. In fact, it's a complete misconception that in order to "dress for success," you have to wear stuffy, boring, or uncomfortable clothing. You're not going to feel uncomfortable—in fact it's the complete opposite. You'll feel more comfortable than you've ever been because you're dressing as the most powerful and confident version of yourself.

The idea is to use your first impression as an element of showmanship. Showmanship is about a show. A transfer of energy. The act of conveying an impression of increase.

The idea behind the impression of increase comes from Wallace Wattles, who wrote *The Science of Getting Rich*. He says, "The desire for increase is inherent in all nature; it is the fundamental impulse of the universe.... Every living thing is under this necessity for continuous advancement; where increase of life ceases, dissolution and death set in at once."

No sale occurs without the impression of increase. You don't buy anything unless you think you'll be better off having it, even if it's just momentarily. If you go to the grocery store and buy gum, it's because you think your life will be better once you have it. More specifically, your breath will be better. Whether you sell yourself or a product, the impression of increase comes from its packaging, merchandising, display, and advertising.

When you make a sale, you help someone. If you're a professional service provider, you can't help a client that hasn't hired you. But your impression of increase can run deeper than just making a sale. The way you package yourself can help you make more money. But it also allows you to help more people.

Here's an example. A few years ago, I hired my mentor. He helped me revamp one of my service offerings, which I then sold to a lawyer. I revamped her image, which ultimately helped her accelerate her own sales cycle. She instantly got more clients, allowing her to serve a larger population of people who needed legal advice. And it all started with my mentor portraying an impression of increase that sold me. That one offering increased the lives of a bunch of people. It became a cycle that increased the life of everyone it touched.

What about you? Do you give off an impression that offers continuous advancement to your potential clients?

What if simply changing your clothes could give you an impression of increase, or attract opportunity?

Just recently, I took my daughter to school and walked out at the same time as one of her classmate's fathers. I was wearing a bright blue dress. You couldn't miss me. I'd actually never really talked to this gentleman before, and he didn't know what I do for a living. We struck up a conversation, and by the time I reached my car, he hired me to work with his wife and later himself. What if I had worn gym shorts like everyone else dropping their kid off at school? I'm sure we would have said hello. But I doubt it would have converted to a sale. Instead, I was wearing a great dress. It made me unique. It made me stand out. It changed the first impression I presented. And ultimately, that dress helped me make money!

That's what a good first impression can do. It can lead to new relationships, new clients, and, most importantly, new sales.

If I told you I had a magic wand that would instantly give you the power and confidence to close more sales, would you take it? Probably! The thing is, I do have a magic wand—and so do you: it's made up of your clothing and overall outward appearance. It's not only a magic wand; it's your secret sales weapon.

Million-Dollar Shoes

One of my favorite examples of the power of first impressions comes from the master of showmanship,

Elmer Letterman. Elmer Letterman is a famous sales tycoon from the 60s. If you can ever get your hands on his book, *How Showmanship Sells,* be sure to buy it, as it's out of print now.

He says, "The most important sale I ever made in my life started with the influence of a pair of my handmade shoes."

While Elmer was standing in a hotel lobby during an event, a complete stranger came up to him and mentioned that Elmer's shoes were the "handsomest pair of shoes I've ever seen in my life." So Elmer offered to introduce him to his boot maker. At the time, most people spent $8 on shoes, including the self-made millionaire Elmer happened to be talking with. Elmer's shoes, however, cost an unheard of $125. He goes on to talk about how, throughout the night, this complete stranger would bring friends over to Elmer's table to check out his shoes. Because of his striking shoes, Elmer built a relationship with this gentleman (Mr. Lefcourt) that ultimately helped him launch his insurance career. The connections Mr. Lefcourt introduced him to, bought $1,250,000 in life insurance in one night. Not bad for a night's work in the 1960s. Not bad for a night's work today!

One of my favorite sayings from Elmer Letterman is, "Opportunities are man-made."

Based on a first impression led by a pair of shoes, Elmer created a $1,250,000 opportunity for himself. Not only did he create the opportunity, but he landed it! He purchased those shoes for $125 and made $1,250,000 because of them. Now that's a heck of a return on investment!

First Impressions Are a Sales Opportunity, Even if You've Already Made the Sale

In my work, clients have often already bought from me before they ever see me face-to-face. When I am finally face-to-face with them, whether it's in person or online, my first impression is a sales tool in three ways.

First, presenting myself well furthers their confidence and belief that they've made a good investment to work with me. They aren't wasting brain activity thinking about whether or not this is going to be a good use of their time and money, and therefore aren't going to ask for their money back.

Second, the first impression I make starts to plant the seeds for future business. Most of my clients stay with me for a few years, so the impression I make is laying the foundation for the extended lifetime value of that client. Let's look at the numbers. Let's say your ideal client pays $5,000 to work with you for their first engagement, but then continues to work with you to the tune of $50,000. That one client has brought in $55,000 in revenue.

If you could simply change the way you dress and easily make a $55,000 sale, it would totally be worth changing your clothes.

Lastly, my first impression also determines whether or not my clients refer me to people they know. People refer professionals that they like and trust. When my client has an amazing experience with me, they will tell other entrepreneurs about it, resulting in increased sales for me.

The Bird Shit Lawyer

Your first impression can have a lasting impact on your bottom line. But just as a great first impression can land you business, a bad one can lose you the opportunity. Let me tell you about the attorney I once worked with but probably won't, ever again–and why.

A few years ago, my husband and I refinanced our house. In order to sign the paperwork, the attorney met us at our house. When I arrived home, there was a white car covered in bird poop parked in my driveway.

I'm an inquisitive person and I am dying to know what happened to his car on the way to my house. Maybe he was attacked by pterodactyls. Or the geese in the pond down the street had an uprising. I'm thinking this will be a great story based on the impressive amount of bird excrement on his car.

So I walk in my house, introduce myself, and immediately ask what happened to his car.

He says, "Oh, nothing. I live downtown and have to park under a tree where birds poop on my car every night."

Needless to say, I'm pretty disappointed in the story. I'd never seen such an impressive display of bird poop on a car, so I was ready for something good.

Our closing begins and he takes us through the necessary steps of paperwork to sign. But the entire time I'm thinking, really? Birds poop on your car EVERY NIGHT and you don't do something about it. You passed three car washes within five miles of my house (the kind you can drive through!), why wouldn't you stop and wash your car?

This guy's car has nothing to do with his ability as a lawyer. Everything went fine with our closing. But none of that really matters, because I will never refer this guy. For starters, I have no idea what his name is. I call him the "The Bird Shit Lawyer." I don't know what firm he works for, which is probably a good thing, because the presentation of his car tainted the firm's overall image for me as well. His first impression killed any possibility of additional sales with me, or the possibility of me referring him to people I know.

Is it fair of me to judge his legal abilities based on the car he drove? Maybe. Maybe not. But I did judge him. And now, instead of telling people to call him when they need to refinance their house, I'm going to send them elsewhere. And maybe tell them a funny bird poop story.

I "thin sliced" the guy, just as the people you meet are thin slicing you. Your first impression isn't just about the clothes you put on, it extends to everything you do (or don't do, like have a great story and a compelling explanation for why your car would be covered in bird poop). If you carry an aura of assurance and success, people will give you credit for an ability to do big things.

People notice the kind of neighborhood you live in, the people you hang out with, the car you drive, where you eat, whether you salt your food before tasting it, and all sorts of other things. In one way or another, everything you do reflects on you and influences the impression you make.

The Bird Shit lawyer's car isn't going to affect whether or not my closing goes smoothly, but it does affect my level of confidence in what I'm buying. When you skip over a massive detail like a car covered in bird poop. I'm now nervous about whether you're skipping over legal details that are going to negatively impact me, and I'm no longer going to do business with you.

What Are People Really Buying?

No matter what you do or what you sell, people are ultimately buying you. That sale is based on the confidence they have in you—or the impression of increase you give. The coolest thing about first impressions is that in most cases, you have complete control over how you present yourself in order to make a great first "sales" impression.

You can't control exactly what the sales person you hired says about your product or service. You don't know what an ideal client will do after visiting your website. But you can help to shape the first impression you make on everyone you meet each day.

Since people believe what they see, you have an opportunity to create an image that attracts the results you want. Your image becomes a sales tool that can easily give you an edge.

What you may not realize is that you're getting a result based on the way you look whether you are trying to or not. Everything in life is getting a result based on the way it looks.

Take an everyday action such as grocery shopping—let's say, for cereal. You grab a box, but then noticed it's dented. So you put it back and get another one. Almost without thinking about it.

Intellectually, you know the taste of the cereal will not be affected by a dent in the box. Yet why risk it when there's a better box you can easily go with instead? The better box gives you more confidence that you'll be satisfied with your purchase. So you put the dent-free box in your cart, and continue with your shopping without giving another thought to putting the dented one back.

Most likely, you chose that particular cereal because you like the taste of it. However, consider how many meetings and thoughts went into what that box needed to look like in order to get you to take it home–so you can decide you like the taste of it.

Every detail of that box was created in a purposeful way, from its design down to the height where it's positioned on the cereal aisle. Have you ever noticed how all the kids' cereal is on the lower shelves? Kids are shorter. That's where they see it, and then convince their parents to buy it.

You don't think for a second about picking one type of cereal over another, or judging a box because it has a dent. But consider: you're the box of cereal. And the way you present yourself can affect everything from whether or not you make the sale to how fast you get seen in an emergency room.

Talk show host Kelly Ripa tells a great story about a time when she passed out while naked, so her husband had to get her dressed before taking her to the hospital.

She arrives at the hospital and has come to and is feeling better, but she's immediately rushed in to be seen by the doctor. She says to the doctor that there are many other people in the waiting room in more pain who should be seen first. He tells her the head nurse gives every patient entering the ER a visual evaluation, and the nurse determined that because of what Kelly was wearing, she must have been unconscious at some point. Therefore, she got priority in the ER.

Her husband had dressed her in a ballet leotard. He said it was just the first thing he saw and, in theory, seemed easy to put on–which is hysterical, because if you've ever had experience with a leotard, you know it's not the easiest thing to get on, especially trying to put it on someone else who is unconscious. So she was wearing a ballet leotard, her husband's soccer pants (the old-school kind that you just snap off), and, the piece de resistance, a pair of red high heels. That outfit alone got her seen ASAP in the ER.

Her story is funny, but it goes to show you how your image really does affect every result you're getting, from how many new clients you get each week to how long you'll wait at the ER.

Your Image Is Your Personal Brand

You want what you like. And you want it to be the best.

In your business, potential clients are making the same quick thin-slices about you as that nurse did in the ER. You do the same thing when investing in products and services for your own business. You purchase what you think will get you the best result. And oftentimes, your decision to pick one thing over another is simply a judgment. Something in your gut tells you which way to go.

So if people believe what they see, you can position yourself in a way that makes working with you the best choice, the best use of judgment. All of this happens through the image you portray.

Let's back up a moment and look at what your image actually is. Your image is a combination of what you wear and how you groom yourself, as well as your nonverbal communication. These three factors combine to frame how people see you.

Even if you don't work with clients face-to-face, your image affects how you are positioned in the mind of your target audience. Your photos on social media, a headshot on a blog post, or the way you look when you meet someone on an airplane are tools that help a potential customer decide if you are someone they want to hire.

People believe what they see. No matter where you are.

Consider your image as your personal brand. You often hear the words *personal branding* thrown around in business as if it's something you need to go out and get, or achieve. But really, everyone has a personal brand, everyone has a certain image–whether you've purposefully created it or not.

Your personal brand is how you position yourself to potential clients. And much of that positioning comes from your image, aka the way you present yourself. Therefore, your image becomes an integral part of creating a personal brand from which you can easily profit.

I had a client who came to me to help him up-level his image, with a goal of getting promoted within six months at the large engineering firm he worked for. We worked together on a Friday, and on Monday he went to work wearing clothes that fit much better and were put together in a fun and interesting way. By 10 a.m., his boss asked him to come speak with him in his office. The way he showed up on Monday–both in the way he looked and in the confidence he exuded–made his boss take notice. His boss told him he was a valuable asset within the company, and wanted to know if he was interviewing for other jobs. He wasn't looking outside the company for a job, but that interaction led to a very candid conversation about his goals and direction within the firm. Within six months, he was promoted.

Up-leveling his image or his personal brand got him noticed by the one person that could help him get to where he wanted to go.

Does Your Image Match Your Opportunities?

Interestingly, a first impression can be positive, without being exactly right for you. Many people make a good first impression. They easily convert sales and, if they're good at what they do, the opportunities around them start to expand. It's that very expansion, however, that can be tricky. Your image must keep pace and be in alignment with your ongoing goals.

I recently asked a longtime client how he felt before we began working together. He said that at that time, he was confident in his ability to deliver what he offered to people—but knew he was in a significant growth phase that would lead to new arenas of opportunity. When he looked at himself and his image relative to the opportunities he was winning, it didn't match up.

You can make a great first impression but if it isn't congruent with what you're trying to do, or sell, potential clients can sniff out that there's something not totally adding up, even if they don't know quite what it is.

Here's a good example. I have a client in the legal industry who entered his career wearing Brooks Brothers suits. He became very successful, growing his business into a multimillion dollar company. His mission is to completely shake up the legal industry so that more lawyers can be happy in their personal lives while still growing a successful law firm. He felt confident and happy. His image had worked well for him up until a certain point. But by the time he came to me, he felt as if something was missing.

Brooks Brothers makes great clothes. But they are designed for someone who wants to feel more conservative and safe—the opposite of his personality. That was the part that didn't match up. His vision is to help people do things very differently than what they have been programmed to do. He does this by teaching out-of-the-box concepts, and by being sort of an out-of-the-box individual. His Brooks Brothers image was far from out of the box. It was very *in* the box.

So we changed the way he was dressing. Since he is on a mission to shake up the legal industry, we shook up his wardrobe. We swapped boring plaid blazers for ones that were fun and full of personality. I found jeans for him that were comfortable, but also looked good on stage. And we found specific shoe designers that not only matched his out-of-the-box image, but became conversation starters with others who coveted the same brand.

You can make a good first impression all day long. But the real question is whether or not it drives the results you're after. If the way you present yourself attracts a client base that will pay $5000 when you charge $50,000, you've got a mismatch that's costing you money.

Each day you have a choice. You can put on garments that simply clothe you. Or you can be strategic about the way you dress and ensure your image will increase your bottom line. The goal for you is to easily present yourself in a way that helps you reach your goals, whether that's a financial goal, lifestyle goal, or a connection goal.

Notice I said the word "easily." This doesn't need to be hard. You don't need to feel uncomfortable. It shouldn't feel laborious. You are simply going to have items in your closet that you can put on quickly in order to feel like the most powerful version of yourself.

If you want to sell a $100,000 client, then you need to look as if you've already landed many of them. You start here and work backwards to discover how to present yourself in an authentic way that will help you effortlessly close sales.

Whether you have a dent in your box, are in the wrong box, or should be thinking outside the box, leveling up your look will take your business to the next level, too.

CHAPTER 2

Gain an Edge in Your Business

The science behind first impressions is fascinating to me. I can geek out for hours reading studies posted in *Psychology Today*. But what I love most is that I know in my heart of hearts that changing the way you dress can change your life. I don't need any kind of study to show me that. I've personally experienced it. I've watched client after client stand a little taller, feel more confident, and surprise themselves by the bigger contribution they make in the world after up leveling the way they look. I realize that sounds dramatic and we're only talking about garments you wear, but it's true. The clothing you put on your body shapes the way you present yourself, and greatly impacts your life. It will give you an edge and, if done right, will easily drive growth and momentum in your business.

Think about this:

You know you're the best at what you do, but how many people are there in your industry that, at least on paper, do the same thing? If you are a consultant, how many other consultants are there? If you're a lawyer, how many other lawyers are there?

It's like the automobile industry. There are a ton of different cars on the market that you can buy. How do you decide which one to even consider? It's the same in your industry. You have to be packaged in a way that makes you stand out, that gives you an edge over everyone else. Otherwise nobody knows you exist.

No matter how big or small your team is, you are their leader. Your job is to go out and win the next client, create the next best product, or be an integral part of a think tank that will result in your next big windfall. Whatever it is, you will win when you have an edge.

Your Business EDGE

In my work over the years I've developed a formula to help you create this edge, and, even more importantly, keep it. This formula offers you an edge to increase sales and get new clients. It's made up of four pieces, and it only works when you have every one of them in place.

The first piece comes from dressing in a way that intentionally engages your ideal client to gain their intrigue and trust.

Next, it's important to dress as if you've already achieved the success or goal you're after. If you're after a $100,000 client, you need to present yourself as if you've already landed many of them—whether you have or not.

Then you have to keep it real. This means that everything you do must be totally in alignment with who you are. The fastest way to lose an edge is to pretend to be something you're not, or to dress in a specific way because you think you *SHOULD*. It's often the things that make you a little weird or quirky that make people want to work with you, so authenticity is key.

Lastly, you have to be consistent in the way you present yourself. Remember, people believe what they see, so if they see you on an off day, that's the impression they'll remember. Consistency is the piece of the formula that helps you keep the edge you create.

By thinking through how you present yourself and using these four pieces, you create an edge for your own self-concept as well as for the momentum of your business.

The EDGE formula is easy to remember:

Engage Your Ideal Client
Dress As If
Get Real
Every Day: Commit to Have Consistency

You're ready to get dressed. Now all you need to do is walk into Bloomingdale's and ask for the section where you'll find clothing to help you engage your ideal client. They would look at you like you were crazy!

Engage Your Ideal Client; **D**ress As If; **G**et Real; **E**very Day: Commit to Consistency. I'm sure it sounds like a bunch of marketing jargon. And in a way, it is, because this entire book is showing you a new way to market yourself—a new way to drive sales.

So rather than simply sending you to Bloomingdale's, let me reverse engineer this for you so it makes it very simple to figure out how to create and maintain an edge that will increase sales and get you new clients.

Engage Your Ideal Client:

Let's start by looking at how you can engage your ideal client simply by changing your clothes. In chapter 1, I said that most first impressions are made before you've even had time to open your mouth. Engaging your ideal client is all about intentionally connecting with them in some way in order to gain their intrigue and trust. I say "intrigue" because in order for someone to engage with you, they have to be intrigued by who you are. Otherwise, you're probably missing out on possible opportunities because people simply aren't motivated to talk to you.

One of the easiest ways to create engagement with potential clients is simply to wear clothing that helps you stand out. The goal is to create an overall image that helps people know you exist, plain and simple. People can't buy from you if they don't know who you are. Remember the idea behind packaging–you are packaging yourself to be noticed.

The idea is not to dress in a way that makes you STICK OUT. When you stick out, you're attracting the wrong attention, like the Bird Shit Lawyer did with his car. You want to dress in a way that makes you STAND OUT to those who might be looking for you. When you stand out to a potential client, they see you as exceptional. You are someone to pay attention to. Suddenly, you have superiority over others simply because you stand out. You are perceived as an authority.

You may be thinking that the idea of walking into a room and having all eyes shift to look at you sounds awful. But that's not what we're talking about. You aren't wearing a clown costume and being shoved into a room full of investment bankers in suits. That would be sticking out, and that's not the goal here.

Think about being a goldfish in a pond. It's an awesome pond, but all the other goldfish are equally awesome. How can you help the person who desperately wants the best goldfish money can buy to *see you*? Being the best doesn't always make you stand out immediately. You have to get the client's attention–in a good way.

A few years ago, I worked with Tyler. He is one of the most dynamic business people you'll ever meet. The first time you meet him, you know it will be a great experience to work with him and that he can take care of whatever you need.

But that wasn't always the case. Tyler had always dressed professionally, including a brightly colored tie to match his outgoing personality, but it still felt like something was missing. Tyler is like a diamond who was dressing as if he were a cubic zirconium. There was nothing wrong with his look, it just didn't make his true potential shine. And so unless you'd had the opportunity to talk to the guy, he didn't stand out.

I revamped his image and polished him up a bit so that he truly does stand out. Not in a wild, weird way. Just as one of the coolest human beings you'll ever meet. Now, before you ever even meet him, you are intrigued by him and want to know more about what he does.

There were two main changes I helped him make to his wardrobe. For starters, I changed the fit of his clothes. By putting him in clothes that fit better (his were a little too big), he instantly gained a sharpness about him that made you take note of him. It made him stand out. The second change was infusing fun into his wardrobe. His big, bold personality warranted clothing that had a little fun and whimsy to them. Again, not clothes for a circus character, but instead button-down shirts with interesting detailing on the cuffs, or a small detail of piping down the placket. Small details that really differentiated him from everyone else.

After working together, he sent me a note thanking me and commenting that he had never put much thought into what message he was conveying to potential clients by how he dressed. Parading out the same black slacks and colored ties made him believe that he was looking the part, but it was just not a match for his outgoing personality. It didn't make him truly stand out.

I have another client in the Southeast, an executive coach for CEOs, who used his image to stand out in a completely different way. When we revamped his wardrobe, we really thought about what would help him stand out to ideal CEOs. For a recent meeting, we put together an outfit for him with one twist: he walked into the meeting with nothing in his hands. No briefcase. No laptop. No iPad. No pen.

Why? He does things differently. That's why CEOs hire him—to show them how to do things differently in order to get the result they're paid to get. In order to stand out, he needed to be just slightly different. Most people would bring a bag with all sorts of stuff. Not because they needed it, necessarily, but because it would present them as prepared. What this particular client needed was his brain, and his ears. That's it. It was a great meeting for him and the act of not carrying around what he thought he "should" was actually very freeing and confidence-building.

The question is, how can you stand out? What could help you intentionally connect and engage with your ideal client or your audience to make them like and trust you? What could you wear to intrigue potential clients without even saying a word?

Dress As If:

Dress as if you've already achieved the result you're after. It sounds simple, but this is the piece of the EDGE formula most often overlooked. Rationally, it makes sense to think that you'll dress better and invest in yourself *after* you achieve the result and have the money to do so. The problem with that thinking is that you may never get there. Instead, when you act as if you've already gotten the result you want, you portray a strong impression of increase.

As an example, let's say you want to land a client who will pay you $100,000. You have to look as if you've already had clients pay you that fee. When you present yourself in that way, your potential clients feel as if you can increase their life in a huge way, and will easily commit to paying $100,000. Remember, no sale occurs without the impression of increase.

If I'm a potential client and you don't look the part, I don't want to be the guinea pig that finds out that you're not actually going to give me $100,000 worth of value. So I'm thin slicing you all over the place to decide if you are a safe bet or not.

You've heard the saying, "Dress for the job you want, not the job you have." It's the same for life, or business, or dating, or whatever your goal is. I recently told a client who is looking to up-level her love life that if she wanted men to stop taking her to Applebee's, she needed to dress as if she always eats at the hottest new restaurant in town. It's the same for your business. If you're working toward a certain revenue goal, you have to dress like you've already made it.

I have a client who is on track to grow her business from the $3 million mark to $20 million over the next four years. She has a plan, and she's working it. And when it comes to her image, there is also a plan for success. She must always dress for where she is going, not for where she is now. Whenever we discuss wardrobe decisions, they are always made by the version of her future self that has already made $20 million. We've even named her future self her "$20 Million Me." Any article of clothing we consider, we look at from the perspective of what her "$20 Million Me" would think about it. Would her $20 Million Me buy this bag? Would her $20 Million Me feel awesome in this dress? If the answer is yes, then we'll buy it. If no, then we know it won't serve her in dressing as if she's already achieved her revenue goal.

There is something important to note here. Acting as if, or dressing as if you've already reached your goal, doesn't mean you have to already drive a Ferrari or only wear Louboutins. If those items are part of your "future me," then I recommend you drive a car that makes you feel as powerful as driving a Ferrari would. Similarly, wear shoes that make you feel sexy and stunning the way wearing a pair of Louboutins would. You are still dressing as if, but you tap into how your "future me" would feel–not necessarily the exact brand your "future me" would buy.

Get Real:

Getting real with yourself is simply about embracing the most authentic version of yourself, from your unique personality to how your body is shaped.

Sometimes authenticity is the hardest thing for you to see for yourself. This is what I'm able to see within my clients. People ask me all the time if I just walk around thinking, "Ugh, you really should dress better." Sure, there are some things I see that do catch my eye, but I really don't see people and judge them as a fashion mess. What I do see are certain people that I meet or simply pass me on the street that I can tell have an impactful presence, but haven't figured out how to authentically portray that on the outside.

Just this week I worked with a woman who is an internet marketing genius. She helps increase clients' revenue by an average of $50,000 a year. She's awesome! She came to me for one reason. Behind the computer she is a maverick, but standing in front of people she would hide. Not literally, but in the way she presented herself. She dressed in a way that nobody ever noticed her because she thought that wearing baggy jeans and t-shirts was authentic to her low-key, low-maintenance self.

Yet when I helped her dig in and discover what makes her truly unique and authentic she discovered her personality wasn't about being low-key or low-maintenance. She was all about being alive, cool, and unique. Sloppy jeans and t-shirts could never help her feel that way. But great fitting sexy jeans with a really fun top and jewelry could! It was fun to watch her literally step out from the shadow and into her truly beautiful self.

When you truly get real with yourself and dress in an authentic way, you have new-found confidence. It comes from really embracing who you are, your unique personality, and knowing how to dress your body shape in order to feel good in your own skin. You look in the mirror and see the lion version of yourself instead of just a cat.

The way you think about yourself shapes every decision you make and every result you get. It's your self-concept. You have to be sure that the person you see yourself as is really who you are.

Before clients work with me, I ask them to fill out a questionnaire. One of the most important questions on the entire thing is this one: What makes you just a little weird?

My dad used to say, "Everybody's weird. It's just your perspective that makes them more or less *weird* in your eyes." What I've learned since is that the kind of things teenagers call "weird" are the very things that make would-be clients sit up and take notice. Your quirks, and the little things that make you weird, are the things that make you most authentic–and more intriguing to potential clients.

I have a client in Charlotte, NC, who loves rubber ducks. Yes, the kind you had in your bathtub as a kid. She has a bunch of them in her office. They are funny and quirky. And they make total sense for her personality, because she's funny and quirky! So she'll never be dressed in something stuffy and ordinary–nor will she dress like a rubber duck. Instead, we make sure her wardrobe hits a professional note in a playful and fun way. We do this by playing with fun patterns that are a little more out of the box, or by using whimsical jewelry to ensure she always feels fun, quirky, and professional.

Embracing your true self sounds easy, but for people who've dressed by the "rules," it can take some practice to find what feels and looks uniquely you. You can invest any amount of money you want on clothing, shoes, or even a new car, but if they don't feel authentic you're simply wearing a costume. When you wear clothing that feels more like a costume, you're actually hiding who you really are. When you dress in a way that truly feels authentic, you'll notice there's an extra skip in your step, you stand taller, you feel prouder. That's the feeling you tap into. Never accept anything less than that feeling.

For example, I recently had a client try on a jumpsuit that she never would have tried on her own. I laughed out loud when she came out of the dressing room because she had morphed into a runway model just strutting her stuff as she showed me the jumpsuit. For her, that article of clothing made her feel amazing, like a model, so it tapped into her true authenticity.

With men, I'm often shocked at how much taller they become when they walk out of a dressing room wearing clothes that are truly right for their personality. Without even realizing it they stand taller and prouder completely changing their presence.

The key is to simply be real with yourself. It's a much easier and fun way to go through life!

Every Day: Commit to Consistency:

This part of the EDGE formula requires a decision—that no matter where you are or what you're doing, you're committed to presenting yourself in a certain way. This is how you'll maintain the edge you've created in your business. When you maintain your edge, you're able to make a significant change to your sales pipeline instead of just landing a one-time sale.

It's about deciding that not only will you look and feel great when you walk into a big meeting, but that you will also look and feel great when you walk into the gym. Instead of wearing the baggy gym shorts and a t-shirt with a hole that you've had for years, you choose sportswear that continues to give you both a mental and business edge. Just to be clear, that means still wearing a t-shirt and gym shorts, but they are strategic, intentionally chosen ones.

There is a challenge to this piece of the puzzle that I'll guide you through. I've analyzed a lot of wardrobes over the years and there's always a common problem. When it comes to clothing, people buy what they like to buy, not necessarily what they need or what will change their result.

Just yesterday, I was in the closet of a high-level executive who loves to go hunting. He loves to buy hunting jackets and hunting pants, and he has a ton of them. The trouble is, he only goes hunting a few times a year. So when it comes to everyday activities like going to dinner with his wife, he has nothing to wear.

His shopping habits were actually acting against his decision to consistently look and feel great each day. He couldn't maintain his edge because he didn't have what he needed in order to do that in all the sectors of his life.

Let me give you a personal example. I love high heels. I like the way they look, and, most of all, I like the way I feel in them. Specifically they make me feel glamorous, sexy, and fun. Yet 90% of my life doesn't make wearing high heels realistic. But it's really easy for me to buy them until I realize they aren't actually going to help me create the image I want with everyday consistency. Yes, I wear high heels. But for those occasions when I know I can't wear high heels, I have to figure out an alternative that is consistent with both my overall image and how high heels make me feel. I simply channel how I feel in high heels (glamorous, sexy, and fun) and find a similar solution that gives me the same mental edge, whether that's a fun flat or a sexy wedge.

Consistency Is Powerful Positioning

When you commit to consistency, it means you present yourself with a certain impression of increase no matter where you go or what you do. It carries over into every piece of marketing you use, from the videos you shoot and your headshot to how you engage with a client in a virtual meeting like Skype—even if you are sitting in your office at home.

In 2011, I wrote my first book, *Simply Effortless Style*. As part of the book launch, I had new headshots taken.

I had my hair done. I picked out a great outfit. I got ready. I went to the studio and took some pictures. I got them back and thought, huh, I don't really look like someone who advises other people on what to wear. Don't get me wrong, they were great pictures. I'm not at all beating myself up about the way I looked.

But the pictures I took simply didn't position me as someone who made you think, man, I need to call this girl. She can help me. So I instantly scheduled another photo shoot and made two changes. First of all, I had my make-up professionally done.

Ladies, I implore you, if you take nothing away from this book take this: never have professional pictures taken without having your make-up and hair professionally done. It makes a world of difference and can save you from paying for double photo shoots.

Men, this is worth asking the photographer about. Under certain conditions, it can be totally appropriate and well worth it to wear a touch of subtle make-up for a professional head shot.

The second change I made was to add personality details to my clothing. My original outfit was fine. But it didn't translate on camera as something that made me stand out. So I added certain accessories that I knew would be in the actual shot. Great shoes didn't do me any good, for example, because unless I was getting head shots for Cirque du Soleil, my feet weren't going to show.

Taking the time to think through your image in every piece of your marketing positions you in a powerful way. Consider how you come across in all facets of your business image. This encompasses your social media presence, your website, the videos you produce, your business cards, and even down to whether or not your car is covered in bird poop! Strive to ensure that all elements of your marketing are consistent with your brand and the direction you're working toward.

Pop over to www.strategicallysuited.com and you can see the before and after headshots I took, as well as get your hands on a really handy checklist to ensure you take amazing headshots the first time!

When It's Right, Consistency Is Easy

In my opinion, the biggest reason people walk around selling themselves short by ignoring the edge they can create for themselves is that they think in order to look good and have a strategic impact, it has to be hard. As in, all of a sudden, it would take an enormous amount of time and effort before you could leave the house. What could be worse than trying to do that every day!?

This book can get you excited about landing opportunities you may currently be missing, but at the end of the day, you'll change nothing if you think that dressing in a strategic way sounds miserable to maintain. I'd actually recommend that you don't change a thing about your image if you're not willing to maintain it.

Don't worry. Creating an edge takes a focused but small amount of effort, and maintaining it is actually quite easy. One of my newer clients recently texted me and said she couldn't believe how easy it was to pack for business trips after working together. She said she was amazed at how little she packed yet how good she looked and felt. It now takes her very little time to pack a suitcase that maintains her edge. To get to that point we did some preparation together but now her closet allows her to easily pack her suitcase, fly across the country, and close her biggest sale.

I've found that most things worth doing require a little work on the front end in order to get the desired result on the other side. As I mentioned at the beginning of this formula piece, all it takes in order to get the result is the decision you want to look and feel a certain way in order to achieve your desired result. So, what's your decision?

If you want to determine how having an EDGE can impact your sales, check out my Image Edge Calculator. It will show you what having an EDGE in your business is fiscally worth to you.

Visit www.strategicallysuited.com to get your results.

CHAPTER 3:

Can New Clothes Really Make You More Money?

You've already heard me say that changing your clothes can change your life. But can buying new clothes really make you more money? I actually guarantee that it will if you are willing to do one thing—invest in yourself.

It feels easy to invest in a book that will help you increase your sales. Or software that will increase your team's efficiency. Or a mastermind program that helps you get to where you want to go. But when it comes to investing in your outer self, sometimes it never occurs to you to open your wallet.

The first time I bought a Louis Vuitton handbag, it felt like a crazy thing to do. I could have bought 20 bags for the price I paid for one. But I decided to buy the bag I really wanted and made the choice to invest in myself. Then a crazy thing happened! On a trip to D.C., a woman stopped me in the airport because she liked my bag and wanted to know more about it (pay attention and you'll notice a lot of unexpected business can take place in airports!!). We talked and exchanged information. She later reached out for help with her presence on stage, and that one engagement more than paid for the Louis Vuitton bag.

The ROI of Investing in Yourself

Neil Patel of Quicksprout.com is a master of making money. He's helped companies like Amazon, NBC, GM, HP, and Viacom grow their revenue. He conducted a year-long experiment to determine whether or not the way you dress impacts your revenue, and he specifically looked at the return on investment.

He tracked everything he did. He changed nothing about his pitch, what he was selling, or the type of business he was after. The only change he made was what he wore. That one change resulted in an increase of sales to the tune of $692,500.

He says that when he dresses nicer, he gets larger business deals. What he wears does create conversations with random people on the street, but his true ROI came from the results he got from dressing nicer in business meetings. As someone who dressed extremely well, he was perceived as someone who was extremely successful–making more people want to be associated with him.

In one year, he spent $162,301 on clothing–and it resulted in a return in investment of $692,500. That's over a 400% return. Not bad, right!? His image gave him an edge. A $692,500 edge, to be exact.

Neil conducted an experiment, but you don't have to. I tell you Neil's story not to encourage you to invest what might feel like an exorbitant amount of money on your wardrobe, but to offer the perspective that when you invest in yourself specifically to create an edge in your business, you will get results.

Neil went big. $162,301 spent on clothing is a pretty big number. But he also got a big return, and I would bet he knew that before ever starting his experiment.

In order to decide to invest in yourself, you need to look at one thing: what's the return on investment you will get? Consider how much a client is worth to you. If a client is worth $10,000, and you spend $10,000 investing in your wardrobe, that one client just paid for your image upgrade. So now, investing in yourself has actually cost you nothing. And anything else that one client buys from you, or other opportunities you now land because of your new image, make that return on investment climb higher and higher.

My philosophy is, since you are going to get dressed each day anyway, why not dress in clothes that help you increase your revenue?

One of my clients came to me to examine how she could use the way she presented herself while speaking to increase her close rate on stage. We spent $5,200 on clothing that she would wear both on and off stage throughout her spring speaking season. During her next engagement, she closed 20% of the room, resulting in $47,000 worth of engagements. And that doesn't include the lifetime value each one of those clients potentially holds. Compare that to her previous speaking engagement, where she closed sales from only 2% of the room and made less than $2,000. Her $5,200 investment with me resulted in a return of $47,000.

You've probably spent zero time standing in a store examining a shirt you might buy and asking yourself, "I wonder what kind of ROI I'll get from this?"

In my experience, it's rare for someone to evaluate his or her closet from the perspective of ROI. Typically, you just evaluate it based on whether or not you've worn something. If you wore it, it was a good investment. If you didn't, then you could have made a better choice.

Each item in your closet works together to create your business edge. So each article of clothing is an opportunity to increase your bottom line. Since each first impression is a sales opportunity, each article of clothing you wear is how you prepare for that conversation—so choose wisely.

The Trickle-Down Effect

There's actually a bigger trickle-down effect that can make an even larger impact on your bottom line than a first impression.

As a leader in your company, you are influencing the way those who work for you dress. I hear all the time, "Oh, you should see the way my boss dresses." As the leader or CEO of your business, you're setting the tone for how everyone else presents themselves to your client, and this has a massive trickle-down effect.

When you aren't dressing your best, your team probably isn't either. Now, instead of just you missing out on potential sales opportunities, you're running an entire organization that is missing potential opportunities to drive sales and company growth.

I live near a dermatologist who has me come to speak at her office each time her team grows or changes. She herself has a very impressive presence, but sometimes clients will come in for a procedure and she isn't the one who sees them. So it is imperative that everyone in her office present themselves in a way that makes them feel their best, but that also portrays the office in the way she has designed it. No one in her office wears scrubs. Everyone has the opportunity to create an image that makes them shine, and that gives their clients the best experience possible. She discovered that when her employees were motivated and given direction on what to wear, they not only looked better, but her client retention increased. Clients enjoyed experiencing an atmosphere where everything and everyone maintains an impression of increase, which is what they are ultimately buying.

I have another client who owns a children's toy store. I frequently work with his management staff to ensure they are dressing in a way that will help with the sale of toys. Many toys sell themselves. But his store is super successful with multiple locations because his staff is face-to-face with the consumer doing product education and driving upsells. He's found that the return on investment to have me work with his staff even warrants giving his staff a wardrobe stipend that I then help them spend. When everyone looks better, all of his stores sell more.

Impeccable Is the Standard

I often work with a retailer called Gwynn's of Mount Pleasant. The store is beautifully merchandised. Their clothes are exquisite. And their service is five star.

Marshall Simon, the owner of the store, is always impeccably dressed. And even though it's rare to walk the floor of Gwynn's and not have the pleasure of running into Marshall, he's not always the person who is selling the customer. He has an entire sales staff to serve his clientele. And his sales staff is also dressed impeccably. Marshall sets the standard, along with a dress code, and it creates an atmosphere of excellence and class that ultimately keeps their clientele coming back.

When You Invest More, You Buy Less

I've found that most of the time, when clients work with me to up-level their wardrobe, they ultimately spend less money—and I think this surprises a lot of people.

There are two reasons for this. First, we always tap into what will give you an edge—and I'm sure you remember that having an EDGE involves only buying things that are truly authentic for you. That alone eliminates 95% of the mistakes most people are making on clothes they buy and then never wear.

Second, I have a very strict policy that if you don't love it, we leave it. That means that if you don't love the way you feel and look in something, it's not allowed to live in your closet. I like to think of the closet as valuable real estate, so don't fill it with things you don't totally love.

I told you about buying a Louis Vuitton handbag. I was surprised that the purchase of that one bag actually stopped me from buying more–and unneeded–bags. I love that one, so I don't need to keep looking for another.

I also encourage my clients to look at clothing purchases as an investment, not just money spent on something to wear. Specifically, you can calculate the cost per wear of something before you buy it to determine if it's an investment, or simply something that will increase your life momentarily, like a stick of gum.

Let's say you need a new pair of shoes. Typically, if you're going to spend more than usual on a pair of shoes, you evaluate that purchase more than you would if you simply walked into Macy's and bought whatever was in your size on the sale rack.

If you spend $100 on a pair of shoes at Macy's and wear them one time, your cost per wear is $100. Plus, if you've only worn them once, you're probably still looking for more shoes, which means you're going to spend more and more money.

Now consider investing in a pair of shoes you're going to wear many times–and they cost $800. If you wear the $800 shoes 10 days out of the month for 12 months, the cost per wear is $6.67. So the expensive pair is actually the better investment. There's more skin in the game, so you're going to pay more attention to what you're investing in and the result you'll get from those $800 shoes.

The idea isn't necessarily to go out and spend as much money on a wardrobe as Neil Patel (unless that's the right strategy for you), but to really think about how what you wear is going to help you create an edge, instead of simply buying what you need to fit in at your next big meeting.

Investing in Yourself Gives You a Psychological Advantage

I mentioned earlier that I know in my heart of hearts that changing the way you present yourself will change your life. It's what gives you the mental edge we talked about in chapter 2. One of my clients said it best: "I now KNOW that in any situation I will be as well-dressed as anyone else who is there." That knowledge gives her–and will give you– mental freedom. It gives you an edge. There's nothing to think about other than walking in, being you, and getting the result you're after.

Michael W. Kraus, a professor at the Yale School of Management, conducted a study in which participants negotiated the sale of a hypothetical factory. His findings showed that clothes with high social status increased dominance and job performance in high-stakes competitive tasks. He said, "In competitive, winner-take-all situations, wearing more formal attire can send others a signal about you being successful and very confident in whatever you're doing. Those more casually dressed, on the other side of the table, tend to back down more easily. Those wearing more formal attire become aware of the respect they are receiving and become more forceful in their negotiations."

The group that was better dressed made a $2.1 million profit on the sale of their factory. Those in the study who were dressed extremely casually only made a profit of $680,000.

This is impactful. They were basically playing a Monopoly game, and were able to affect the results they got based on wearing gym clothes or a suit. Imagine what could happen with your clients and real money when you invest in yourself.

Investing in yourself is also good karma. If you're in business, you're asking someone to invest in you, a product you've created, or an idea you have. At the end of the day, you have to be willing to invest in yourself if you want others to invest in you. It's just good karma!

Whether you believe in karma or not, there is something to be said for the fact that how you do anything is how you do everything. If you're not willing to invest in yourself other people sense that, and won't be willing to invest in you. It's a mismatch.

Consider what you do. Do you ask people to step up and be the best version of themselves? If so, in order to stay in integrity, you have to do the same thing for yourself.

The Key to ROI Is Your Decision

I have a client who flew all the way to Tokyo just to buy the clothing she thought she wanted. She loved how Harajuku girls dressed, and had adapted elements of that into her own style. For those not familiar with Harajuku, it's not only an area in Tokyo, but an international fashion trend that pairs different fashions together—such as the punk look with the schoolgirl uniform. The result is a wacky representation of individuality that looks more like a doll than a professional. Not your typical dress for someone running an almost million-dollar company.

Her goal was to soar over that million-dollar milestone in revenue, but the Asian-inspired Harajuku look was too cute and cliché to help her drive momentum in her business. Even though she loved the clothing she bought in Tokyo, she realized her purchases were actually causing her to miss out on business opportunities. People looked at her as someone who was fun and different, but not somebody they were necessarily eager to hire.

So she made a decision. She would no longer buy things just because she was drawn to them or thought they were fun. She decided to only invest in clothing that would help her gain the sales momentum she was after. Based on that decision, she hired me.

Through me, she got the help she needed and now buys clothing that still feels fun–and even has the occasional nod to her love of Harajuku style–but that looks more professional. Her new style helped her sail straight to $3 million in revenue.

Neil Patel made a decision to spend a lot of money on clothes in order to discover the ROI he could get.

I make a decision every day to put on clothing that will get results, instead of items that simply act as garments.

Elmer Letterman, in my favorite book, *How Showmanship Sells*, said it best: "Creating a prosperous image isn't nearly as difficult as making the decision to do so."

All you need to do is make a decision. Everything else will fall into place.

CHAPTER 4

The Trap of the Perfectly Good

I f you're like most people, nobody really taught you how to dress. There probably wasn't a class growing up in school called, "Wear This to Make a Great Impression," or, "Wear This and You'll Make More Money."

Instead, how you present yourself and what you wear developed over time based on the opinions of your Mom or Dad, a spouse, or friends; what you see in the media; and/or what you see in the stores where you shop. Basically, a melting pot of random influences both positive and negative have shaped the way you get dressed each morning–and, ultimately, how your customer perceives you, both good or bad.

I recently worked with a client who came to me because his business was growing by leaps and bounds, but he was struggling to maintain an image that embraced both the growth of his business as well as the logistics of owning six successful Little Gym franchises. His business requires that he travel often by car. He is in the gym with his customers on a daily basis. And he is the leader of an amazing team that teaches classes to children each day.

We talked through the logistics of a typical day and his goals around how he wanted to present himself in order to maximize the impression he makes. But his biggest aha came when we were talking about what had shaped his dressing decisions in the past, before hiring me.

I asked him if there was ever a time in his life when he got to decide what to wear and why. The immediate answer to that was, "Sure! I dress myself every day. Obviously, I decide what I want to wear."

But when he really thought about it, he realized there was never a point in his life where he had personally mapped out the way he wanted to present himself. When he was younger, his mother purchased his clothes. As an adult, he bought whatever he needed in a pinch and then married a woman who enjoyed shopping for him. Which was great, because he wasn't interested in spending time shopping. Unintentionally and over time, those outside influences became why he presented himself the way he did, and that no-decision decision caused him to miss opportunities to inspire his team, acquire new clients, and feel really good in his own skin.

Dressing in a way that was perfectly good was holding back his success. There's nothing wrong with the items his wife purchased, or the way his mother taught him to dress. Everything he learned and bought was perfectly good. It just wasn't excellent, nor was it on target.

In business, perfectly good won't cut it. You don't aim to provide just perfectly good customer service. You didn't build a product that was only perfectly good. You want growth and momentum, and perfectly good doesn't drive sales.

When it comes to yourself, it's really easy to accept presenting yourself in a way that is perfectly good. You'll get by. You'll make the sale. You won't see a decrease in your numbers this month. But you won't see exciting momentum or an increase in revenue either, for one reason: when you fall into the trap of accepting what's perfectly good, you no longer have an edge.

Perfectly good is what happens when you leave any number of pieces out of the EDGE formula, and it happens more often than you might think.

The Race to $1 Million

There is an event planner I know who is well known in the coaching industry. Her company covers many events I also attend, so over the years, I've gotten to know her and see her on a regular basis. I watched and noticed that as her business grew to the $1 million mark, the way she presented herself actually declined. She no longer looked fresh and energized. Most importantly, she no longer presented herself as the best event planner money can buy.

There was nothing wrong with what she looked like. She is a beautiful woman. But the sparkle and shine that highlighted her dynamic personality and positioned her as the event planner you wanted if you were hosting an event, had disappeared. Her clothes looked fine, but they were a few years old and didn't help her stand out from anyone else in the room. She lost her edge.

She's a great example, because note that I said she "lost" her edge. When I first met her, she had it. Yet as her business grew, she got really busy and forgot about the last E in the edge formula, Every Day: Commit to Consistency.

I get it. When you hit it hard, you don't have time to spend hours finding the perfect thing to wear, or to figure out which clothier can make you the best shirt. You're busy! But simultaneously, you lose both your mental edge as well as the edge that positions you in your ideal client's eye as their go-to person to buy from. Eventually, that dulling of your edge can run your business into the ground.

When you're growing your business very quickly, at what point do you take time and revenue to invest in yourself?

It's like the age-old question of what comes first, the chicken or the egg. But in business, in order to make money you have to spend money, particularly on yourself. So the answer to when you should invest in yourself and stop accepting perfectly good is: RIGHT NOW!

Thank Goodness, It Fits!

I called this chapter the Trap of the Perfectly Good because it's a subtle trap, and one you can unknowingly fall into. I never asked her, but I'm sure that deep down, my event planner friend knew she wasn't presenting as her best self. But what if you don't know what your best self looks like? You're stuck in a "perfectly good" trap without even knowing it can be better. To you, it's just what life looks like. This happens a lot when it comes to finding clothes that fit.

Without a doubt, one of the biggest challenges of creating an image that is strategically suited can be finding clothing that fits you properly. Size is one of the first areas where people settle for what's perfectly good without even realizing it. In fact, 90% of people are wearing clothing that is actually too big.

The fit of your clothing can make or break the way you present yourself. If it's too small and you're a woman, you are looked at as being too provocative. If you are a man and your clothes are too small, people assume you're lazy. But when you wear things that are too big, you come across as sloppy, frumpy, and the farthest thing from successful.

You'll be shocked by this, but my most challenging client to source the right things for is a woman who is a size 0. She's that coveted tiny size, a 0, so you'd think it would be easy. But here's the kicker. She's tall. Almost everything in a size 0 is made for people under 5'4". So a dress that looks professional on most size 0 women looks like we have a different agenda on her, because it's too short. I have to get creative by finding brands that are specifically made to be tall as well as sourcing the right seamstress to create some of the wardrobe items we need.

The same is true when you fall into what retail considers to be a plus size, for women. Or Big, for men. The reality is that you have to be more creative, look in more places, and, if you are doing mainstream shopping, you are stuck with a smaller selection than your friends who fall into what retail considers a more mainstream size. Is this fair? Nope. But it doesn't mean you settle. You stay true to what gives you an edge. That's going to yield far better results than buying whatever happens to sort of fit off the rack. It may mean that you have clothing made. Or that you get creative in how you put an outfit together in order to create the image you desire.

It can feel really frustrating, but here's the deal: retailers aren't out to get you. They are in business to make money. We all are. If you can't support yourself, then you can't help anyone else, because your business won't exist.

Designers create sizes based on the proportions of their target market. When they design a garment, it's fitted to a model that resonates with their target market. And then sizes go up and down from that starting point. That's why when you try three jackets on in the same size by different designers, they can all fit completely differently. It can make it extremely frustrating to try and find clothing that ticks all the boxes of your image edge criteria. But just because it's a challenge doesn't mean you settle on something that will just sort of work—or be perfectly good.

If you were designing a new website and your web designer kept presenting you with a site that seemed just okay—just good enough—you wouldn't accept it and move on. You're going to do whatever it takes (research, consulting other designers, multiple iterations, etc.) in order to create a site that gets you the results you want.

It's the same with your clothing. Laying the foundation, or having someone help you lay the foundation, will always get you the result you're after. Perfectly good will just get you a closet purge a year from now, along with the same sneaking suspicion you're missing out on opportunities and need to buy clothes all over again.

Twice a year, I run a retreat during which an intimate group of high-level professionals gather with me to up-level their image in just two days. At one of these retreats, I met a woman named Donna. Donna had been settling for what felt to her like forever—even though she is seriously one of the coolest people you'll ever meet. Powerful, dynamic, a serious ball buster, and a very special human being, she had never been able to develop her image edge because she was settling on clothes that simply fit her body. If something fit, it was a success, so she stopped there even though it was only perfectly good.

Yet in her professional life, Donna never stops. She's a kick-ass criminal defense attorney. If you've done something really stupid, you want her on your side. Conversely, you don't want to be against her. There's no settling. Perfectly good would never fly in court. Only winning.

After attending my event, Donna went from accepting what was perfectly good to tapping into what gave her a real edge.

Before coming to me, she knew she was in a rut. About her clothes. About her message. About her attitude and her appearance in general. She knew she needed a change. During the retreat, she learned how to dress her shape to be most attractive as well as secrets about her personality she didn't even know. The part that made her unique. The part that other people see as special, but she had overlooked. She learned how to incorporate her quirks into her image, instead of as something she thought she had to hide.

But my favorite part is that she said she felt like a whole new person. That she was unchained from her old self and was free to laugh and dream and smile. She became more accessible to her clients, which was and is the whole point.

People told her she'd lost weight. They asked if she had a face lift. They thought she had colored her hair. And the best part was when we sent her husband her before and after pictures, he said he thought he had a mistress.

Check out Donna's pictures (they're so good!) at www.strategicallysuited.com. And if you haven't already, grab my **Picture Perfect Checklist** to discover how to take your own perfect headshots. You'll also get access to information on any upcoming style retreats if you want to learn more about the process Donna went through.

Time Marches On

No one in business will remain successful unless they accept the inevitability of change.

Henry Ford, the country's first billionaire, almost ran his company into the ground because he didn't want to change his once-successful policy of stamping out automobiles in only one color and style.

In many ways the ability to change is the key to success. Particularly when it comes to age.

Age can be an ironic disqualifier in business. One day you look too young, and the next day you look too old. And it's a big trap that I see people falling into when it comes to accepting what's perfectly good. It ultimately leads to a decrease in relevance and a decline in revenue.

The way you present yourself when you're in your 20s will not produce the same result as when you are 30 or 40. The suits you wore when you took the business world by storm in your 40s will not keep you relevant in your 60s.

When you cling to an image that you created five or even 10 years ago, you're unintentionally telling your audience that you are perfectly good. Which works fine, until someone else stands in front of them who portrays themselves as perfectly awesome. All of a sudden, your audience is paying attention to someone else.

This isn't about trying to stomp out any competition; this is about maintaining the edge that your image provides you no matter what your age.

Anyone Can Help You Be Perfectly Good

When it comes to getting dressed, anyone can help you figure out what to wear.

You can find everything you need in order to up-level your image on your own. There are amazing stores with wonderful customer service that can help you. There are companies like Stitch Fix or Trunk Club that will send you a wardrobe in a box. You could even ask your wife or husband or a friend to help you shop. And all of these things will work—sort of.

The secret to driving the success of your business isn't simply putting on nice clothes. The secret comes from creating an image that gives you an edge. It ensures that you are always strategically suited to get to where you want to go.

Many of my clients have tried these convenience solutions and have found they don't really work if your goal is to increase sales and get new clients. They fix the problem of wondering what to wear each morning, but it doesn't make you stop wondering if you're missing possible opportunities in your business. It's a Band-Aid, not a strategy to create an edge.

One of my clients in the Washington, DC, area tried all of these convenience sources before working with me.

She tried Stitch Fix. She tried Daily Look. And both of those resulted in a few wardrobe items she kept, but none that gave her an edge. She had worked with a stylist in the past, but had grown past the stylist's abilities. She made an appointment with a personal shopper at Nordstrom. She had a fun experience and bought some nice clothes. But something was missing. She wasn't on the right path.

For me, it was easy to see. She had left out the "**G**"(Get Real) part of the EDGE formula, the part that makes her most authentic. Most of what was in her closet missed the mark on the most important part of her personality: this outside-the-box, funky, badass, you'll-never-meet-anyone-like-her quality. In order to get that, you need more than just a solution for making shopping easier. You need someone who is on your team and is ready to ride the same growth express train you're on. Someone who sees a shift you need to make before you do. Someone who shows you the truth of the bigger picture.

What's the Truth?

At the end of the day, my real job is to tell the truth. I am a truth teller with a bird's-eye view of how to boost your bottom line. Your friends won't tell you the truth. Your family won't tell you the truth. Not because they don't want to, but because they can't see the entire vision to be able to tell you if something is the right or wrong direction. They can't see if something is just perfectly good.

When I work with my clients, we are constantly evaluating if something is working or not, and that's how we know it's right. I know they are going in the right direction. So instead of spending months heading down a path that may or may not result in opportunity, we just get straight to the task and create an image that gives them an edge in a matter of days. That way, they can quickly get back to what they do best.

It will come as no surprise that I spend a lot of time in dressing rooms while clients are trying on clothes. And I can't help but overhear what others are saying. People, particularly women, will come out and ask a friend for their opinion. And you can always tell that the friend either doesn't know what to say, or will just straight up lie to keep from hurting her feelings, or will help her justify to the moon and back why she should buy something—whether it's a good decision or not.

I want you to be able to see the truth in terms of how something truly can serve you, both personally and in your business. That's what makes a piece of clothing an investment instead of simply something you buy. It's what takes something from perfectly good to exactly right.

If it's not right, it doesn't give you an EDGE. And without an EDGE, you're selling yourself short.

When you no longer accept what's perfectly good in your life, you bridge the gap between landing opportunities and wondering where they are.

CHAPTER 5

The Freedom of Success

Your next step is to make a decision. Will you activate your sales edge and boost your bottom line? Or will you continue as you are without an edge and accept just perfectly good? Only you can make this decision. And the key to a successful decision is to give yourself a deadline. By when do I want to have this EDGE?

Otherwise it will look something like my recent experience: I decided at the beginning of 2016 that I wanted to write my second book and have it published at the start of the fourth quarter. Months went by, during which I wrote a little, fiddled with my outline, and mostly ran myself around in circles while accomplishing essentially nothing.

I knew I could write a book. In fact, I've already written a book, this would be my second one. So there was no question I could do it on my own.

But here's the deal. I wasn't doing what I needed to do in order to get the result I wanted. Time was ticking. So I made a decision. I set a deadline. I hired Angela Lauria of Difference Press to help me do it by July 7, 2016. As I write this book, I'm sitting in the Author Castle of Difference Press, and I'm holding myself accountable. And man, it's so much easier. So much more fun. And a hell of a lot better than it would have been if I had done it on my own.

We all have an area of expertise. Even though I am an author and have even written a book prior to this one, my expertise is not how to write a book. My expertise is helping you discover how to use your image as an edge to boost your bottom line.

For me, hiring Angela was well worth the investment I made. The book hasn't even published yet and I've already recouped my investment.

The question is, what would having an edge be worth to you?

If you speak on stage, what would it be worth if you could close half the room instead of zero?

If up-leveling your own image inspired your team to do the same, how could that affect your company-wide sales?

If you could easily close people you run into in the airport, what would that be worth?

If you're ready for an edge, when would you like to start using it? Put a date on it and let's make it happen!

The Real Point of This Book

In my opinion, the real reason to read this book is to increase your sales. Sure, you're also going to look and feel better. You'll be strategically suited. But what I really want for you is to make more money so you can make a bigger impact on the world, spend more time with the people you love, and be able to do what you've been put on this earth to do.

One of my clients in North Carolina was put on this earth to be an amazing father, husband, mentor to CEOs, and a host of other things. He is an executive coach for high-level CEOs whose fees start at $100,000. He'd flown to Detroit in the middle of the week to pick up his daughter from summer camp when he ran into a CEO he had been targeting over the last couple of months. He was on "dad time," so he was dressed casually in a t-shirt and jeans. But even though his dress was casual, he made sure he very much looked like a guy that CEOs hired for a fee of $100,000 all the time. He looked powerful and confident, even though he was wearing a casual shirt and jeans. That run-in was the opportunity he needed to get on that CEO's calendar, and ultimately led to landing a new client.

The point of this story isn't just that his image helped him land new business. Part of the reason he was intriguing and attractive to this CEO was that my client nailed his own impression of increase. He couldn't have advertised himself any better. His overall image gave him an edge. The CEO was schlepping to a meeting five states away from home. My client was just being dad, flying first class with his daughter on a Tuesday. He embodied success. Success that was so good, it was no big deal to be flying around the country on a Tuesday with his daughter. That kind of freedom and success is exactly what that particular CEO yearned for, so working with my client was a no-brainer after that day.

My client made a big sale, and that's awesome. But the best part is he now has the opportunity to affect the life of that CEO, maybe even the relationship the CEO has with his own daughter. And that is very cool. All of this happened because my client accepts nothing less than maintaining his edge, and he knows that when he is the absolute best version of himself, amazing things happen on many different levels.

The Surprise Secret

There's kind of a surprise secret at the end of all of this. At the end of the day, the power of your image is less about the physical articles of clothing you wear, and more about how you feel in what you wear.

Superman always wears a cape to maintain his edge. Batman drives the Batmobile. Rhonda Rousey braids her hair in a very particular way in order to tap into her fight mindset.

I have a client who drives a red Corvette. She feels amazing when she drives that car, so we use it as a metaphor for her entire life. When she walks into a big meeting, she feels the same power and exhilaration she gets from being behind the wheel of that Corvette.

All of these things are what transform them into the best version of themselves. It's that quality that compels clients to talk to you and helps opportunities to show up. It's what builds your momentum, gives you an edge on your competition, and helps you live a life that truly makes a difference.

If I braid my hair, I won't believe I'm a fighter. If I put on a cape, it won't make me feel super. It would be fun to drive the Batmobile, but frankly, I'm just too practical to figure out how to fit my two kids, dog, and husband into it.

But if I step on stage, I'll always be in a dress. ALWAYS. Why? It makes me feel powerful. It helps me be my best self and serve my audience in the best way. It's an item of clothing that gives me an edge.

And that's what I want your image to be for you. A secret weapon that attracts amazing opportunities to you, but also allows you to be free and confident no matter what the day brings.

Remember my client Donna? She told me that the greatest gift her image transformation gave her was simply feeling free. She no longer had to bother thinking about all of this other stuff that had weighed her down in the past. She was no longer trapped by made-up rules in her head about what she could and couldn't do. Or who she could or couldn't be. She could just be herself—one of the coolest and powerful women I've ever met.

Amazing things can happen simply by changing your clothes. Change your clothes and see!

Taking the Next Step

So, what's next for you?

You love the idea of using an edge to generate growth and sales, so now it's time to change your clothes.

But your next step isn't to run into your closet and purge everything you own. Or jump into the car and go buy new "edge-worthy" clothes.

Step back and examine where you want to go in your business, and ask yourself if you have the edge you need in order to get there.

If there is a gap between where you are now and where you want to go, then let's talk!

If you're like most people, you're simply missing a piece of the puzzle that is hard for you to see on your own.

If you're ready to use your edge to grow your business, then I invite you to reach out and request a consultation with me. Together, we'll examine what an edge is worth to your specific business and what your next step should be.

To get started, go here: www.strategicallysuited.com

I look forward to talking with you.

All the best,

Lee Heyward

ACKNOWLEDGMENTS

When I was in third grade, my parents built their dream house (which was really a farm!)–including a barn to house my Dad's antique cars. My dream since I started riding horses at five years old was to have a horse of my own, so by the time I was in middle school, the cars had been kicked out and horses moved in. I am grateful for every minute I spent scooping poop, throwing hay bales, and learning how to be a responsible and self-sufficient individual. My parents instilled in me and my siblings that anything is possible as long as you're willing to think a little outside the box. And for that life lesson, I am forever grateful, Mom and Dad.

Andrea and Alex, it always has been and will be a really fun ride! Thank you for your support, and for the fact that I know we are always there for each other.

***

Rome wasn't built in a day, and neither was my business. I've had the guidance of amazing mentors along the way, a few of whom I want to acknowledge here.

Julio Blanco, you started me on the path of possibility and reminded me to simply embrace who I am and just roll with it!

David Neagle, you changed my life simply by saying two words to me: Why not?

Ron Wilder, I am grateful to you for always holding me to a higher place and believing that I will get there.

Cristina Strunk, you showed me how much fun being a grown up can be. Without you I wouldn't be where I am today.

Michelle Salater, I'm forever grateful we landed in the same BNI meeting on the very same day. This journey has been so much fun with you and I'm honored to learn from such an amazing friend every day.

***

Growth is the key to business and much of mine is the result of Marshall Simon and Weezie Hiott taking a leap of faith. You taught me that it never hurts to ask, and the relationship we've formed has changed my life and my business. I thank you for that.

***

Fourth grade really can change your life. It's then that I met Kristen Caroline, who was my first guinea pig and continues to be the best friend a girl can have.

***

Although I don't know you, Stacey London and Clinton Kelly, your show, *What Not to Wear*, inspired me to start my business. Without you, it wouldn't have occurred to me to start the career I love so much.

***

There are times in life when the stars simply align, and that happened when I met Angela Lauria. Thank you for your amazing expertise and process.

Maggie McReynolds, thank you for your support and push to be the best version of myself.

And thank you to Morgan James for bringing my book to life.

***

In my opinion, marriage is one of the most challenging and rewarding things you can ever do. I am so grateful to my husband, Brian, for his constant support and kindness, and the reminder that you can never assume.

Parker and Davis, you are amazing human beings who teach me life lessons every day, and for that, I thank you.

***

When I started my business in 2007, I never imagined the amazing people I would meet along the way who would greatly impact my life. For that I am so grateful, and am reminded daily that it's the people you know that shape your life for the better. I am extraordinarily lucky to know and be touched by all of you.

ABOUT THE AUTHOR

Style strategist Lee Heyward helps clients create an edge to grow their sales and get more clients. Lee believes that when you up-level your image, you confidently close every sale, stand proudly on stage, and achieve the results you desire. Her real-world approach demonstrates that up-leveling your image isn't about creating a perfect package; it's about tapping into what makes you the best version of yourself for both you and your clients.

At a young age, Lee discovered the importance image plays in your success. When her best friend entered a new school in fourth grade, she put together all the outfits she should wear in order to nail a "cool kid" first impression.

As a sales representative for an equestrian footwear and apparel company, Lee quickly learned that the way you package what you sell is key in order to get the result you're after. In 2007, she launched her company to help entrepreneurs discover how easy it can be to increase their bottom line simply by changing their clothes.

She is the author of her first book, *Simply Effortless Style: A Real Woman's Guide to Making Style Easy and Fun.*

Lee lives in Charleston, SC, with her husband, two children, dog, and cat.

To learn more about Lee, visit www.leeheyward.com.

THANK YOU

I pinch myself each day that I have the opportunity to help people like you change their life simply by changing their clothes. I'm truly honored you chose to read this book.

There are a few resources mentioned throughout this book that are listed here for easy reference, and available at www.strategicallysuited.com.

Your Image EDGE Calculator – Use this easy tool to see what it is worth in your business to create an image edge.

Before and After Photos – Check out some of the before and after shots from my clients' transformation.

Picture Perfect Checklist – Use this handy guide to ensure you take the perfect headshots the first time!

Or, if you're ready to talk about what an EDGE can do for you and your business, reach out to schedule a time to connect with me at www.strategicallysuited.com.

Morgan James makes all of our titles available
through the Library for All Charity Organization.

www.LibraryForAll.org

Printed in the USA
CPSIA information can be obtained
at www.ICGtesting.com
JSHW080001150824
68134JS00021B/2218

9 781683 502432